100 T

for

Writing for

Film

and

Television

Introduction

When I first decided to take a sabbatical from writing for mainstream TV to focus on other projects, a number of writer friends warned me of the madness that can overtake the solitary novelist. Writing for telly is a sociable business; I can't think of any other art forms where you're invited on a weekly basis to sit in a small office and be congratulated on your brilliant work as foreplay to an eight hour diatribe on why you have to rewrite every word.

Assuming I was going to miss such merry social interaction, these friends suggested I perhaps teach a course, work with new writers, share my experience. I made a few enquiries, and with a true writer's soul, decided that teaching looked like a lot of preparation and hard work – in short, *a proper job* - and thus wasn't for me. What did strike me during my research however, was how many people *were* teaching writing and charging what seemed to me to be staggering sums for doing so. What really galled me though was how little actual writing experience a lot of the people running the courses actually had.

So, on a wet August afternoon, I idly set up a Facebook page called Script Doctor, offering to help people with their scripts for the meagrest of fees. To attract interest, and to keep myself amused, I posted a 'tip' on the first day and recklessly called it 'Tip For the Day'. Having given it that title, it felt ungainly not to post another the next day and pretty soon those writer friends of mine were laying odds that I couldn't keep it up for a year, Monday to Friday *(Do you get the impression I should get some new friends?).* And now, five months in, here come the first 100.

This is *not* a writing course; there's no structure or reasoned plan. These tips come pretty much at random from flaws I see on screen, in scripts that I'm sent, and most of all from my own early drafts. It's not meant to be read in any particular order; it's for dipping into when inspiration is low; a time-wasting device that will let you convince yourself you're still working when really you're just idly flipping pages. This book is meant to sit on your desk, in your laptop bag, or in that most important sanctuary for any writer, the bathroom.

By necessity, each tip is short. When I started, Facebook had a 240 character limit which offered my crossword-loving mind the challenge of constructing haiku-like nuggets of advice. For purity's sake, I've left them pretty much unedited. Enjoy, and happy writing.

SCRIPT DOCTOR, JANUARY 2010

Many new writers think they can get by on inspiration and imagination, but writing is as much a craft as it as an art. Anyone can make a table out of four posts and a plank; a talented artist could even make a beautiful table from them, but unless you know how to dovetail joints and calculate weight and form, it'll just fall down. You may have the art, but you still have to learn the craft.

The hardest part about writing is not inspiration, it's filling the pages. Whatever your other work/home commitments, set a realistic timetable to write as often as possible and stick to it rigidly. It's a job - treat it like one.

Ray Bradbury wrote 'Throw up in the morning, clean up in the afternoon'. In other words when you sit down, forget style, accuracy, structure and character. GET THE WORDS DOWN. Then take a break, print it off and read it. I find it helps to change environments, (a fancy way of saying 'go to the pub') then look at your work with an editorial eye, make notes and implement them slowly and precisely.

It's highly unlikely that your script is 100% original; learn to identify your influences and subconscious plagiarisms before someone else spots them.

When two people are in conversation they rarely use each other's names. SO DON'T DO IT IN YOUR DIALOGUE. Before your final polish, do a 'find' search through the whole script for each character's name and delete any clangers. If you think it's a minor point, try a conversation with a friend using their name in every sentence and see how ridiculous and wearing it is.

Some days it's just as hard to stop writing as it is to start. Find a strategy to switch off when writing time is over or eventually you'll lose your mind. Get away from the keyboard and live a little.

Keep an eye on structure if you're running three or more consecutive plotlines. At 2nd/3rd draft, break down each scene of each plotline into a two line precis, print them out on different coloured papers (a colour for each narrative). Cut them into strips, one strip per beat. Lay them down in the order of your script - at a glance you'll see if you've left too long between beats

Your opening scene; it's usually the one you fall in love first, but be prepared for it to be the first scene you lose. You won't have found the rhythm, pace or voice yet.

When writing a character who's significantly older or younger than you, write a short timeline for them set against events from history. For some reason many writers think they're 19 whatever their real age. As a result they give children their own memories of things that happened before the character was born, or vastly exaggerate the memories of their older characters.

Quirk alone is not story. Sure, make your characters fresh and original but don't sacrifice credibility in favour of quirky. Remember how annoying those eccentric types can be in real life - why should it be any different on screen?

Swearing does NOT make a script adult. A well placed expletive, or a string of them can hammer home a point beautifully, but characters who f and b throughout are usually repetitive, tedious and unlikeable. As with any rule there are exceptions but it's the exceptional writer who can break the rule. Try writing 'clean' dialogue with real emotional power. It's much harder to do but far more effective.

Lord Reith had it right: 'educate, inform, entertain'. Learning the latter is tough, the first two you can do something about. Keep yourself educated and informed and show it in your work.

Beware postmodernism; the writer as character, the breaking of the fourth wall and the parallel timeline can all be very effective but all too often comes across a puppeteer showing his strings. It distances the audience and you risk losing their empathy with the characters.

How far will your hero go? There's a strict ratio between the sins committed against your hero and the sins they can be forgiven for while still maintaining hero status. Don't lose the viewer's sympathy with a disproportionate response.

Coincidences; sure they happen in real life but in a script they can look sloppy especially if overused. Try and engineer interactions and events logically rather than rely on coincidence.

There's a fine line between a seed and a signpost. Every element of your dénouement has to be seeded but be subtle. Make the seed too obvious and it becomes a big glowing signpost giving away your climax.

Your central characters should all have a clearly defined goal or desire in the opening scenes. The goal may change and they may never achieve it but we have to know what they want from the very beginning, even if it's only that they don't know what they want.

If one of the characters in your scene isn't speaking, acting or reacting, then why are they there? Sounds obvious but you'd be surprised how often people leave a 'spare wheel' in their scene.

Networks looking for writers on established shows won't read 'spec scripts', i.e: your own attempt at an episode. They want to read original pieces where the story and characters are your own and they can get a feel for your 'voice', so don't send that fantasy episode of Eastenders in. (Of course once you're accepted, they'll do as much as they can to stifle that voice, but that's another story).

There are as few original magic tricks as there are original stories. Watch good stage magicians to see how they use character, narrative, props and settings to create a new twist on an age-old device.

If you're not actually on a commission and struggling to motivate yourself to fill the pages, ask a friend to be your deadline fairy. Choose someone you love, respect and would hate to disappoint and make a deal to deliver a realistic amount of pages once a week. They don't have to read them, just be there to count the pages and nag you if you blow the deadline.

Dialogue howler: 'business' - as in 'none of yours'/'well I'm making it mine' or 'mind your own business'/'it is my business'. Tired and lazy - bin it.

Expositional dialogue is bad at the best of times, but between two characters who both already know the information, it's unforgivable. Married couples don't remind each other what they do for a living, technical experts don't explain to each other how the equipment they're using works. Don't do it - find a better way.

Sports and games. If you don't know them, don't write them. Bad poker games, ludicrous football exploits, darts in soaps; too often just cringeworthy.

Stationery is your friend. Post-it flags are a joy for tracking your plot structure. Ascribe a different colour to each strand or character and mark each page where the strand appears, 'stepping' the flags down the edge of the script like a ladder. When you're done you'll be able to tell at a glance if your beats are evenly structured.

What's in a name? Think hard about your character's names. Do they fit their age and social background? Avoid alliteration unless you want them to sound like superheroes.

Be wary when writing children. It's way too easy to slip into simplistic speech patterns and the liberal use of 'mummy' and 'daddy'. Kids have complicated syntax, bizarre imaginations and scattergun levels of vocab. Make them real, not dolls - it'll make your script far more interesting.

Dialogue horrors; Using 'Let's just say...' as a pre-emptor to deliberate sinister or comic understatement. 'Let's just say he won't be needing his shoes for a while', 'Let's just say she won't be getting married in white'. It's lazy and horribly over-used - avoid it.

Consider the geography of your story. Is it deliberately claustrophobic or have you accidentally written scene after scene in tiny rooms? Are you expressing man's insignificance in the face of nature or just writing a lot of people talking in fields? Think about the effect on the viewer of moving from interior to exterior. Think visually.

If you intend to place your protagonist in an original and unusual form of peril in your final act, it's a good idea to demonstrate how the peril works and the true horror of its effect on a random bit-part character in the first act.

That fateful moment when the tragic news is delivered? Try and write dialogue for it, even if you only capture the crushing mundanity of grief. The longshot of unheard conversation through a window, the dropped cup, the crumpling knees and silent fall to the floor, the 'it's Frank...' followed by a cutaway – all very powerful but actually writing the scene is a much greater challenge.

Your subplot or guest story isn't just there for cutaways and to tell a second story for supporting characters; it should mirror the action and emotional dynamic of the main story, giving a strengthening subtext or an alternative standpoint.

Beware the pun; they're fun in everyday conversation, but rarely sit well in dialogue. More dangerous still, a well-formed pun can sidetrack your imagination for hours into planning entire series or movies simply around your punning premise. Avoid the pun as a title at all costs, unless you're titling sitcom episodes where it's just about acceptable. Shun the pun.

As an exercise, extrapolate a complex plot from small random incidents. That knife dropped that missed your foot by inches, the collision with a random stranger. Consider all the possible ramifications if things had gone just slightly differently - you never know where your imagination could lead you.

The 'pathetic fallacy' is aptly named. Rain is not a character, nor is it a substitute for generating genuine suspense or sympathy. Used well, the weather can become a worthwhile plot device, just don't make it your default position for setting atmosphere or character mood.

That nasty chunk of expositional dialogue you can't avoid? If two or more characters know the information you need to get across, have each of them explain it in smaller chunks to another person, intercutting between them. That way the visual is changing, and you can reveal character thru their delivery - particularly useful for those police interview scenes.

That all important 'love at first sight' scene. You could just make it plain that they have something unusual in common and have them remark on it ('You like Bogart? So Do I';). Far better though is for them to fall effortlessly into the shared jargon/catchphrases/language of their mutual vibe without them overtly mentioning it.

Classic dialogue howler. No-one in real life repeats the last word of a sentence when they've been told something that shocks or baffles them. If you spot this in your script you're in trouble....
'trouble?'

A good fight scene is one of the hardest things you'll ever write. Pitch the skill of the fighting to the experience of your characters and the reality of your script. Remember too the aftermath; the level of your script's reality determines how quickly your characters recover. Cheat on this and you've lost at least half your audience - is it worth the risk for two pages of action?

Ticking clocks are not just for time-bombs. A set deadline or ultimatum in your script is a simple way of adding a sense of urgency to your story, even if it's just a train to catch to get the girl/boy - as long as you keep throwing obstacles in the way, of course.

Mentally soundtrack your projects. When I'm working on a number of different things, I pick one CD to fit the mood of each and play it constantly for a particular piece. When I have to make that awkward mood switch from comedy to crime drama or script to prose, changing the CD helps me to get into the different headspace required smoothly and quickly. Especially useful first thing in the morning.

Your voice is always going to come through in your dialogue but sometimes that can lead to characters sounding the same. If you're having trouble creating a fresh voice for a character, think of a friend you know and ascribe the character their speech patterns, nuances and turns of phrase.

If you have an ensemble cast with three or more characters of roughly equal importance, you can give a good early demonstration of their personalities by seeing them react to an event in different ways. It could be as a simple as a pretty woman walking by, or as big as a car crash or fire. Use their reactions to give an early guide to who they are.

Don't be despondent if at the end of the day your script is fifteen pages shorter; you've probably done more work and been more productive than if it were twenty pages longer.

What's your story for? You don't have to have a 'message', but you do need to have a solid purpose, even if that purpose is simply high octane entertainment. Read your fourth draft and examine every scene to see if it accomplishes your goal or gets across your central tenet. If you're simply writing to sell a script, without a clear overview of what your script is, you'll fail.

What are the broad themes of your script? Identify them for yourself then highlight them with smaller devices and images that run throughout the plot. Be subtle though; nobody wants to see the emotional manipulator who's hobby is puppetry.

Film and television are two very distinct and different story-telling languages. Film allows a scope for silence, focus, complexity and concentration that doesn't always work in television. If you're writing for TV (and sometimes for film, too) try and make every scene about more than one thing, even if it's just using the location to cross two stories over.

Another dialogue howler. All too often, 'I almost forgot' followed by a key piece of information simply means 'The writer almost forgot'. The only time its excusable is if your character is dropping a killer piece of information that he's been deliberately sitting on in order to score points for a maximum hit. Even then it's a cliche.

That fabulous twist ending you thought of? It's not enough to carry a script unless you've got a solid story that everyone can understand too. No-one will care about your smart-ass ending if they don't care about the people involved. Make sure your story holds up with or without the tricksy pay-off.

Try not to run more than an hour or so over your allotted daily writing time (Unless that time is horribly short anyway). There's a difference between 'being on a roll' and 'being unable to stop typing long after the creativity is exhausted'. Those extra hours could wind up in losing the next morning to editing and deleting.

Write that uncommissioned first draft as if you had a 30 million budget, then take a break and read it with a producer's head on. Whatever they say about respecting story, most producers have a pocket calculator in their head totting up the bill and the higher it goes, the more they panic about cost. Maybe ditch that six helicopter crash in the opening scene for something cheaper to film. Besides, solving those problems will make you a better writer, more reliant on story and less on spectacle.

Dialogue howler - 'by the way' is too often used in dialogue as a weak link between two unrelated lines (or awkwardly at the end of a scene when you've just realised the characters have forgotten to introduce themselves). Just as a script has structure, so should a conversation; make those segues effortless and natural.

No-one says 'I love you' at the moment they fall in love. Show the moment without using the line - it's probably the most insincerely over-used phrase on the planet. Do your best to avoid it (unless of course your character is lying) - almost any other line of dialogue will convey the moment if you've set it up right.

Research is great, but don't let it dominate. It's essential you do your homework, but too many writers, having putting in the hours at the books, then feel the need to throw every second of that reading into their plot and dialogue whether it's relevant or not. The solidity of the world you recreate from your research should feel effortless and natural, not smug and pretentiously 'educational'.

When dealing with worlds or environments of the imagination, find the commonplace details of everyday life to draw the audience in to your characters and situations. If you don't, they'll feel cold and distant and the audience won't identify. Luke Skywalker had to finish his chores, Spielberg symbolised alien abduction with mashed potato, Harry Potter has homework to do.

Exposition is never harder to write than when explaining away the mechanics of that scientific anomaly/ooglymoogly monster/haunting. Avoid the protagonist's insane deductive leap, shun the found ancient tome of lore conveniently explaining the whole kaboodle and eschew the shambling idiot savant who holds the key. Find logical and plausible ways to explain your dynamic.

In fantasy fiction, it's very tempting to give your superhero/villain, ultimate mage/fighting machine, ubervamp/cosmic warrior omnipotent powers. Don't. The minute a hero is presented as indestructible, all jeopardy disappears. Likewise, if you cast your villain as unstoppable, you're cheating the audience when you eventually have to stop him. This is why Batman always works better dramatically than Superman.

In SF, fantasy and horror, establish otherworldly rules and mechanics early - the kryptonites and crucifixes, the super-strengths and occult powers, the magical rules and technological capabilities. Once they're established STICK TO THEM. You can't just use them when it suits the plot, you have to create a solid internal reality and breaking your own rules undermines the illusion and weakens the drama.

Carry two notebooks, a small one for jottings, one-liners and random loglines for the future, the other one A4 for detailed structures and mapping out the project you're currently working on. This helps keep your immediate work focused in the big book and the smaller book will either feed to the future or just act as a recycle bin for 'bad' ideas.

Scars, missing body parts and wheelchairs are NOT shorthand for evil. I can't believe I still see this offensive nonsense on a regular basis on mainstream TV and cinema. It's not only discrimination its shockingly lazy writing (and people with learning difficulties are not constantly adorable or blessed with insight into the future).

Create private jokes, rituals and language between characters who are emotionally close. If you embed them in the audience's mind, they can become a great gutwrenching punch for that big heart-rending scene where otherwise you may have to resort to cliche or generalisation.

Personalise your characters for yourself and your audience with props both physical and mental. Even if you never use it in the script itself make a list of what they would have in their pockets or handbag on an average day, ask yourself what they drink in the pub, how they sit in company and how they sit alone, what's the first thing they eat from the fridge? Solidify them in your head.

Stanislavsky's not just for actors, especially
when it comes to his theories on emotional
memory. When you come to those big scenes of
anger, loss, love, jealousy or despair, take a short
while before you start writing to remember
those moments in your life. Tap into your own
memories.

When writing a thriller, the audience should
usually learn things before the protagonist,
never the other way around. It's okay for both
audience and hero to be in the dark for a while,
and it's okay for them both to learn things at the
same time, but the hero should never
consciously know something the audience
doesn't. It's cheating.

Sex in drama is a lot like football in drama - never as exciting or convincing as the real thing. Does your sex scene really advance plot or enhance character? Or is it just there to appear adult, a cheap trick to attract viewers or worse of all, something you've thrown in because you're bored of the sound of your own voice? If so, stop at the bedroom door - we all know what sex is.

An antihero without a likeable personal trait is just a villain, a hero without a flaw is a pain in the arse.

Throw in a surprise in your opening fifteen minutes and another at the end of your first act/end of first episode. It can be as simple as an unexpected visual or location or as huge as killing the star. As much as you need to establish 'a contract' with your audience, you also need to let them know you're ready to break that contract.

Look out for homophones, rhymes and possible mispronunciations in your dialogue. Get some friends together and read it aloud. This weekend alone I've heard a character repeat 'You're in' three times, spotted an accidental rhyming couplet in Phantom Menace and heard a cockney say of a deceased recluse 'he literally shat himself away'.

Just because it was powerful, scary and moving as hell when you woke up, doesn't mean that dream you had was a great idea for a story. Get it down in your notebook by all means, but don't dash straight to the keyboard to formalise it. It's like knitting steam. Clear your head, watch the News or something, then get back to yesterday's job in hand.

Try not to get 'married' to anything in your script. You may have started with the-fabulous-scene-that's-the-best-thing-you've-ever-written, but by the time you've finished first draft, you may have a script that works pretty well BUT for that scene. Dump it mercilessly, you can always use it again. If you don't you'll spend draft after draft ruining a good script to make it work.

The 'dream sequence' is often a nightmare -
they rarely film well, they smack of pretention
and they're usually an excuse for lazy story-
telling. If you're considering one, ask yourself
what purpose it serves. The language, imagery,
pace and lighting of dreams is so intensely
personal that it's almost always doomed to fail.

Sometimes it's hard to learn from great drama
because great drama hides its tricks and
techniques so well. It's well worth watching a
little crappy TV from time to time because the
creaks and leaks and saggy bits are all on the
screen to learn from. An episode of Murder She
Wrote or Diagnosis Murder can teach you a lot
of what to avoid.

Even more so than drama, every sitcom has its own strata of reality, be it real, hyper-real, drama-real or surreal. Unlike drama, you cannot stray outside that level - you can't mix and match. The Royle Family can do 'human', 'My Hero' can't. They have their own world, own rules. It sounds simple, but a lot of scripts don't grasp this and fail.

Two of the key links in the chain of almost every comedy, especially sitcom, are pomposity and innocence; more precisely, pomposity pricked and innocence victorious. Ollie, Capt Mainwaring, David Brent, Father Ted/Stan, Pike, Tim, Father Dougal. It's a blessing and a curse – a solid archetype to work with but a legacy that makes it hard to find a fresh and original take.

In sitcom, all the rules of drama still apply, but in a more magnified way; this is especially true when it comes to dialogue and character-voice. The distinction of speech-patterns for each character is heightened; consider Blackadder Goes Forth and the radically different deliveries of Blackadder, Baldrick and George.

Like most good horror, the majority of great sitcom is dependent on close and inescapable confinement - whether it be something obvious like Porridge or Red Dwarf, or a deeper emotional trap like the family ties of the Steptoes or the economic bond of The Office, these people cannot escape their situation. Lock your characters into the world you create.

When writing a sitcom or comedy series, too many people think the 'sit' is the actual occupation or location. Think deeper - the 'sit' is much broader; it's their 'situation'. So Dad's Army is comedy of class and generation gaps, Teachers says 'work in a school, you stay as a kid'. That's the deeper dynamic, location is irrelevant.

A good title is a nightmare to find; Lines from literature are almost exhausted (though it's still worth a thumb through a dictionary of quotations). Titles tend to have certain rhythms. As an exercise, spend an hour without a story in mind, trying to construct dramatic sounding titles - it'll help in the future when you need one and may even inspire you to a whole new story.

There's a quirk of human physiology in the muscles of the face; when we're close to the moment of tears and trying to hold them off, an unexpected laugh will tip us over into sobbing. Use it - build your big emotional moment then find just the right gag to nail it home.

Surreal imagery can make for astonishingly powerful visuals but don't use it for its own sake. A weird scene on its own can be horribly self-indulgent, but if you work to seed and explain all the elements that come together to make the image then you won't be robbing the audience.

If you just can't avoid that dialogue-heavy scene, take the edge off it by giving the characters plenty of physical 'business'. Have them on the move, or in a setting with visually engaging props to work with, something to keep the eye happy while the ear takes in the information.

It may sound trivial, but this is an incredibly common error I see all the time. Check your spelling slowly and by eye; spell check won't help if your typo is a word in its own right. If you can't spell, ask someone who can to read it. Poor spelling makes you look amateur (not to mention the loss of dramatic edge to lines like 'she lay helpless as the bat-like creature hoovered above her throat').

Story inspiration can come from pretty much anywhere, but it never hurts to give it a nudge. Build up a personal stock set of texts to browse regularly, not to steal ideas, but to trigger them and find ways in to the tale you want to tell. I use the Old Testament, Fortean Times, Brewers Phrase and Fable, Peter Carey's short stories and the Penguin Dictionary of Saints - choose ones that suit you.

If character A tells character B a useful piece of exposition or plot-advancing information, we don't need to see character B tell character C and bore the audience with it again. Come in at the end of the scene and just see C's reaction (unless, of course, there's a strong emotional reason for doing so).

It's not enough to know your characters inside out - you also have to know how they feel about each other. 'Put a microphone' in front of each character and ask them about the others in turn - try and write a single, working line of dialogue that reveals both the speaker's main character trait AND their opinion on the character they're discussing. It makes a handy addition to a pitch doc' too.

Avoid the Deus-ex-Machina. Your ending has to be a surprise, but it shouldn't be a bewildering one that comes from nowhere. Your finale can be as wild and out there as you like, as long as you've planted the seeds and clues that justify it. Even 'Magnolia' prologued with an examination of surreal phenomena.

Exclamation marks are for exclamations and only for exclamations. Use them sparingly in dialogue and NEVER in stage directions - if your stage direction needs an exclamation mark to convey a sense of drama then it's a poorly written sentence - fix it.

Characterisation is all about empathy; finding common ground between character and audience, no matter how small. This especially applies to your bad guys. You don't have to make them likeable, but there has to be some sort of touchstone between them and the viewer; otherwise the whole thing goes pantomime.

The days of the Remington typewriter and Tippex are long gone, but I still see a lot of scripts with a plain 'courier new' cover page and just a title and author name. Use your title page as a pitch-poster; choose an appropriate font, find a good picture and throw your log-line across the bottom. Producers open dozens of these a week - make yours stand out.

Look for moments of dramatic and/or emotional resonance between your A story and your B story (you do have a sub-plot, don't you?) and try and juxtapose and intercut at those points. If your hero is celebrating with champagne for instance, is your B-story character drowning their sorrows alone at the same time?

Don't base the 'truth' of your characters and story on something you saw in a movie. Even if you're writing SF, fantasy or period, whatever the genre, make the central tenets of your narrative and protagonists true to what you know and believe about the world and humanity.

Get in late, come out early. When you start a scene, the natural inclination is to open with your protagonist walking into the room and to stay in the scene until he leaves. You only need the meat of the scene - come in on that, and get out when the important stuff's been said and done - the hello's and goodbyes just kill the pace.

If someone says they don't understand something in your script, it's 99 % certain your script isn't clear (unless they're an idiot, in which case, why are they reading your script?). It's supreme arrogance to assume that its because they don't 'get it'. Listen to why they're confused, don't try and explain, just fix it (unless of course its an early beat that's going to pay off later).

Learn to recognise your own cliches. Even if you avoid the common ones, you'll find the more that you write, the more you repeat certain figures of speech, phrases and phrasings, unique to you. Fine if you only do it with one character and remain consistent, but if every character's using them, it clangs on the page. Identify them, Write them down and do a 'find' search at editing time.

A good editor is like a best friend whereas your relationship with the script is like a naive lover. You'll coddle and spoil it and be blind to its imperfections (even when its obviously cheated with someone else in places). Your friend will be the one to give you perspective to recognise its faults.

You've finished a draft of your script. Print it off, take a break for a few hours, get out of the house. Then sit down, pen in hand for your edit - if at any point you feel the need for a coffee, make a note on whichever page you're on (I usually draw a coffee cup). Odds are that if you got distracted at that point, there's something wrong with that part of the script.

When dialogue sizzles and sparks it's great, but when the conversation's dull or clanking or full of exposition, it stinks. As an experiment, look for ways to write your scenes in silence, use props and action as dialogue. It's a golden rule because it works - Show Don't Tell.

Understatement and subtext carry your fraught emotional scene far more powerfully than 'the big speech'; there's true pain to be wrought from the mundane minutiae and everyday phrases. In two hours of watching home-shot footage of 9/11 last night, a small quiet gut-wrenching moment of a woman three blocks away, filming the tragedy, her voiceover to her crying infant - 'go back to sleep honey, it's nothing'

Subverting the audience's expectation gets harder and harder as we become more sophisticated. The obvious twist is exactly that; obvious. Constantly strive to genuinely surprise your audience.

Learn the Rules. Then Break Them All

2253025R00029

Printed in Great Britain
by Amazon.co.uk, Ltd.,
Marston Gate.